The NFL's Greatest Teams

BALTIMORE RAVENS

Big Buddy Books
An Imprint of Abdo Publishing
abdopublishing.com

Katie Lajiness

abdopublishing.com

Published by Abdo Publishing, a division of ABDO, PO Box 398166, Minneapolis, Minnesota 55439.
Copyright © 2017 by Abdo Consulting Group, Inc. International copyrights reserved in all countries. No part
of this book may be reproduced in any form without written permission from the publisher. Big Buddy Books™
is a trademark and logo of Abdo Publishing.

Printed in the United States of America, North Mankato, Minnesota.
092016
012017

THIS BOOK CONTAINS
RECYCLED MATERIALS

Cover Photo: ASSOCIATED PRESS.
Interior Photos: AP Images for NFL (p. 25); ASSOCIATED PRESS (pp. 5, 7, 9, 11, 12, 13, 14, 15, 17, 19, 20,
    21, 22, 23, 25, 27, 28, 29); Allen Kee (p. 18); Damian Strohmeyer/Associated Press (p. 7).

Coordinating Series Editor: Tamara L. Britton
Graphic Design: Michelle Labatt, Taylor Higgins, Jenny Christensen

Publisher's Cataloging-in-Publication Data

Names: Lajiness, Katie, author.
Title: Baltimore Ravens / by Katie Lajiness.
Description: Minneapolis, MN : Abdo Publishing, 2017. | Series: NFL's greatest
    teams | Includes bibliographical references and index.
Identifiers: LCCN 2016944871 | ISBN 9781680785289 (lib. bdg.) |
    ISBN 9781680798883 (ebook)
Subjects: LCSH: Baltimore Ravens (Football team)--History--Juvenile literature.
Classification: DDC 796.332--dc23
LC record available at http://lccn.loc.gov/2016944871

Contents

A Winning Team

The Baltimore Ravens are a football team from Baltimore, Maryland. They have played in the National Football League (NFL) for more than 20 years.

The Ravens have had good seasons and bad. But time and again, they've proven themselves. Let's see what makes the Ravens one of the NFL's greatest teams.

Black, purple, gold, and white are the team's colors.

League Play

The NFL got its start in 1920. Its teams have changed over the years. Today, there are 32 teams. They make up two conferences and eight divisions.

The Ravens play in the North Division of the American Football Conference (AFC). This division also includes the Cincinnati Bengals, the Cleveland Browns, and the Pittsburgh Steelers.

Team Standings

The AFC and the National Football Conference (NFC) make up the NFL. Each conference has a north, south, east, and west division.

The Pittsburgh Steelers are a major rival of the Ravens.

Fans love to wear wacky outfits to home games.

Kicking Off

   In 1995, Cleveland Browns owner Art Modell moved the team from Cleveland, Ohio, to Baltimore. The team changed its name to the Ravens. They played their first game in 1996. The Ravens had a losing record their first three seasons.

   The team hired Brian Billick as head coach in 1999. The next year, the Ravens won 12 regular-season games, two play-offs, and the AFC **championship**. Then they played in the Super Bowl and beat the New York Giants 34–7!

The Name Game

The Ravens are named after a bird in a famous poem by Edgar Allan Poe.

The first Ravens game was played in front of 64,124 fans! The Ravens beat the Oakland Raiders 19–14.

Highlight Reel

During the early 2000s, the Ravens had many ups and downs. In 2001, the team went to the play-offs but lost. The next year, the Ravens had a losing record. In 2003, the Ravens won their first AFC North Division title. But, they lost in the play-offs.

John Harbaugh became the team's new head coach in 2008. He got the Ravens back on track again. They made the play-offs four years in a row! Sadly, they did not make it back to the Super Bowl.

Ravens fans get excited to cheer on their team!

Jamal Lewis (31) was the fifth overall pick in the 2000 draft.

Then, in 2012, the Ravens finished the regular season with a 10–6 record. They beat two teams in the play-offs and won the conference **championship**.

In 2013, the Ravens earned a trip to the Super Bowl. There, they beat the San Francisco 49ers 34–31. They were Super Bowl champions again!

The Vince Lombardi Trophy is awarded to the Super Bowl winner.

Ravens players received championship rings after they won the Super Bowl.

Defensive back Chykie Brown celebrated the Super Bowl win by laying in the confetti!

Halftime! Stat Break

Team Records

RUSHING YARDS
Career: Jamal Lewis, 7,801 yards (2000–2006)
Single Season: Jamal Lewis, 2,066 yards (2003)
PASSING YARDS
Career: Joe Flacco, 28,322 yards (2008–2015)
Single Season: Vinny Testaverde, 4,177 yards (1996)
RECEPTIONS
Career: Derrick Mason, 471 receptions (2005–2010)
Single Season: Derrick Mason, 103 receptions (2007)
ALL-TIME LEADING SCORER
Matt Stover 1,464 points (1996–2008)

Famous Coaches

Brian Billick (1999–2007)
John Harbaugh (2008–)

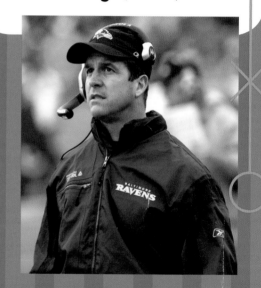

Championships

SUPER BOWL APPEARANCES:
2001, 2013

SUPER BOWL WINS:
2001, 2013

Pro Football Hall of Famers & Their Years with the Ravens

Jonathan Ogden, Tackle (1996–2007)

Fan Fun

STADIUM: M&T Bank Stadium
LOCATION: Baltimore, Maryland
MASCOTS: Poe, Rise, and Conquer
TEAM SONG: "The Baltimore Fight Song"

Coaches' Corner

Brian Billick took over as head coach in 1999. He started to build a powerful defense. By 2001, the Ravens were Super Bowl **champions**!

In 2008, the Ravens hired John Harbaugh. Harbaugh became the first NFL head coach to start his **career** with five straight play-off appearances. In 2013, he led the Ravens to their second Super Bowl win!

Billick coached the Ravens for nine seasons.

Harbaugh believes team work is the key to success.

Star Players

Jonathan Ogden TACKLE (1996–2007)

Jonathan Ogden was the team's first-ever **draft** pick in 1996. He was chosen to play in the Pro Bowl 11 times in a row. This is the NFL's all-star game. Ogden is the first player to spend his entire **career** with the Ravens.

Matt Stover KICKER (1996–2008)

Matt Stover joined the Ravens in 1996. He had his best season in 2000. Stover scored every point for the Ravens in five straight games. He helped the Ravens make it to the 2001 Super Bowl. Stover is the team's **career** scoring leader with 1,464 points.

Ray Lewis LINEBACKER (1996–2012)

Ray Lewis was part of the powerful Ravens defense. He helped the team win both Super Bowl titles. Lewis was named the NFL Defensive Player of the Year in 2000 and 2003. He was invited to play in the Pro Bowl 13 times.

Jamal Lewis RUNNING BACK (2000–2006)

As a **rookie**, Jamal Lewis helped the Ravens win their first Super Bowl. In 2003, he rushed for 295 yards in one game. That was an NFL record at the time. Lewis finished the season with 2,066 rushing yards and was named NFL Offensive Player of the Year.

Todd Heap TIGHT END (2001–2010)

Todd Heap played offense for the Ravens for ten seasons. He was a fan favorite. Every time he caught the ball, fans would cheer "Heeeapp!" Over the years, he caught 467 passes for 5,492 yards. Heap also made 41 touchdowns, which is a team record.

Ed Reed SAFETY (2002–2012)

Ed Reed was a record-setting defensive player for the Ravens. During a game in 2008, Reed intercepted a pass and ran it 108 yards for a touchdown. That was an NFL record! Reed also holds the team record for most **interceptions** with 61.

Terrell Suggs LINEBACKER (2003–)

Terrell Suggs was selected as the tenth overall pick in the 2003 **draft**. He was named the NFL Defensive Player of the Year in 2011. Suggs is a six-time Pro Bowl selection. And, he holds the team record for the most sacks.

M&T Bank Stadium

The Ravens play home games at M&T Bank Stadium. It is in Baltimore. The stadium opened in 1998. It holds about 71,000 people.

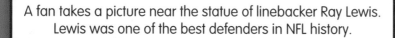
A fan takes a picture near the statue of linebacker Ray Lewis. Lewis was one of the best defenders in NFL history.

M&T Bank Stadium is 185 feet (56.39m) tall!

Go Ravens!

Thousands of fans flock to M&T Stadium to see the Ravens play home games. In 1998, the team got a **mascot**. Poe is a raven. He helps fans cheer on the team.

The team also has two live ravens named Rise and Conquer. Rise and Conquer make special appearances at home games.

The team's marching band is called the Marching Ravens.

As of 2016, Poe is a seven-time Pro Bowl mascot.

Rise and Conquer weigh only 1.5 pounds (0.68 kg), but their wingspan is 3.5 feet (1.07 meters)!

Final Call

The Ravens have a long, rich history. They won Super Bowls in 2001 and 2013. Even during losing seasons, true fans have stuck by them. Many believe the Baltimore Ravens will remain one of the greatest teams in the NFL.

Ravens players cheer for their teammates after great plays!

Through the Years

1996
The Baltimore Ravens play their first season.

1999
Owner Art Modell sells the team to businessman Stephen Bisciotti.

2000
The Ravens go to their first play-offs. They beat the Denver Broncos 21–3.

2002
Safety Ed Reed blocks the first punt in Ravens history.

2001
The Ravens beat the New York Giants to win their first Super Bowl. Ray Lewis is named Super Bowl MVP.

2003
The team's stadium is renamed M&T Bank Stadium.

2006

The Ravens end the regular season with a team-best 13–3 record.

2008

On September 7, John Harbaugh wins his first game as an NFL head coach. The Ravens beat the Cincinnati Bengals 17–10.

2011

For the first time in team history, the Ravens win all the regular-season games against their AFC North rivals.

2013

The Ravens beat the San Francisco 49ers to win their second Super Bowl. Quarterback Joe Flacco is named the Super Bowl MVP.

2015

The Ravens have been a team for 20 years. They wear special patches to honor two decades.

Postgame Recap

1. What is the name of the stadium where the Ravens play home games?
   A. U.S. Bank Stadium   **B**. M&T Bank Stadium   **C**. AT&T Stadium

2. Name the single Ravens player in the Pro Football Hall of Fame.

3. How many Super Bowls have the Ravens won?
   A. 0
   B. 1
   C. 2

4. What are the names of the team's two live mascots?
   A. Rise and Conquer
   B. Kick and Punt
   C. Poe and Paul

Glossary

career a period of time spent in a certain job.

champion the winner of a championship, which is a game, a match, or a race held to find a first-place winner.

draft a system for professional sports teams to choose new players.

interception (ihn-tuhr-SEHP-shuhn) when a player catches a pass that was meant for the other team's player.

mascot something to bring good luck and help cheer on a team.

rookie a first-year player in a professional sport.

Websites

To learn more about the NFL's Greatest Teams, visit **booklinks.abdopublishing.com**. These links are routinely monitored and updated to provide the most current information available.

Index